Our Catholic Identity™

CATECHISM WORKBOOK

Grade Five

Ed DeStefano
Author

RESOURCES FOR CHRISTIAN LIVING™

Allen, Texas

> "The Ad Hoc Committee to Oversee the Use of the Catechism, National Conference of Catholic Bishops, has found this catechetical series to be in conformity with the *Catechism of the Catholic Church.*"

President: Kim Duty
Publisher: Maryann Nead
Catechetical Advisor: Jacquie Jambor
Editorial Director: Ed DeStefano

Contributors: Judy Deckers, Nancy M. DeStefano, Anne Battes Kirby, Margherita Rader, Dee Ready, Kate Sweeney Ristow

Production Manager: Jenna Nelson
Senior Editor: Joan Lathen
Project Editor: Judy Deckers
Editor: Linda Hartley
Senior Production Editor: Laura Fremder

Art Director: Karen Malzeke-McDonald
Page Design: Laura Fremder
Cover Design: WaveBase 9, Carol-Anne Wilson

NIHIL OBSTAT
Rev. Msgr. Glenn D. Gardner, J.C.D.
Censor Librorum

IMPRIMATUR
† Most Rev. Charles V. Grahmann
Bishop of Dallas

July 3, 1997

The Nihil Obstat and Imprimatur are official declarations that the material reviewed is free of doctrinal or moral error. No implication is contained therein that those granting the Nihil Obstat and Imprimatur agree with the contents, opinions, or statements expressed.

20205	ISBN 0-7829-0738-5 (Student Book)
20235	ISBN 0-7829-0785-7 (Annotated)

2 3 4 5 6   03 02 01 00 99

ACKNOWLEDGMENTS

Scripture quotations are from the New Revised Standard Version of the Bible, copyright 1989 by the Division of Christian Education of the National Council of the Churches of Christ in the USA. Used by permission. All rights reserved.

Excerpts from the English translation of *Rite of Marriage* © 1969, International Committee on English in the Liturgy, Inc. (ICEL); excerpts from the English translation of *The Roman Missal* © 1973, ICEL; excerpts from the English translation of *Rite of Penance* © 1974, ICEL; excerpts from the English translation of *The Ordination of Deacons, Priests, and Bishops* © 1975, ICEL; English translation of *A Book of Prayers* © 1982, ICEL. All rights reserved.

Photos: Robert Daemmrich/The ImageWorks, 43R; Full Photographics, 63, 72, 75; Jeff Greenberg/Unicorn Stock Photos, 43L; © Bill Wittman, 6, 70; Larry Kolvoord/The ImageWorks, 50; SuperStock, 20

Illustrations: Laura Cavanna, 29; Paula Lawson, 35; Karen Malzeke-McDonald, 7, 15, 47, 59; Bob Niles, 31, 49; Jennifer Pickett, 9; Margaret Sanfilippo, 19

Copyright © 1998 by RCL • Resources for Christian Living™

All rights reserved. No part of this book shall be reproduced or transmitted in any form or by any means, electronic or mechanical, including photocopying, recording, or by any information or retrieval system, without written permission from the Publisher.

Send all inquiries to:
RCL • Resources for Christian Living™
200 East Bethany Drive
Allen, Texas 75002-3804

Toll Free   800-822-6701
Fax   800-688-8356

Visit us at www.rclweb.com

Printed in the United States of America

Contents

PART ONE: We Believe

1. **The Gift of Faith** 6
   Faith, Nicene Creed, Creeds
2. **Sacred Scripture** 8
   Sacred Scripture, Bible
3. **Sacred Tradition** 10
   Sacred Tradition, Apostles, Magisterium
4. **The Mystery of the Holy Trinity** 12
   The Holy Trinity, Blessings
5. **God the Father, Creator** 14
   Creator, Image of God, Divine Providence
6. **Jesus Christ, Our Lord and Savior** 16
   Christ, Messiah, Lord, Savior, Incarnation, Paschal Mystery
7. **The Gift of the Holy Spirit** 18
   Holy Spirit, Easter, Ascension, Pentecost
8. **The Marks of the Church** 20
   Marks of the Church, Names of the Apostles
9. **The People of God** 22
   People of God, Hierarchy, Laity, Consecrated Life, Bishop, Priest, Deacon
10. **Mary, the Mother of God** 24
    Virgin Mary, Immaculate Conception, Assumption

Review: We Believe 26

PART TWO: We Celebrate Our Catholic Faith

11. **The Liturgy and the Sacraments** 28
    Liturgy, Sacraments
12. **Sacraments of Initiation** 30
    Baptism, Confirmation, Eucharist, Grace
13. **The Mass** 32
    Holy Sacrifice of the Mass, Liturgy of the Word, Liturgy of the Eucharist, Transubstantiation, Blessed Sacrament
14. **Sacraments of Healing** 34
    Sacrament of Penance, Sacrament of Anointing of the Sick

15. **Sacraments at the Service of Communion** 36
   Sacrament of Holy Orders, Sacrament of Matrimony
16. **The Liturgical Year** 38
   Advent, Christmas, Lent, Easter Triduum, Holy Thursday,
   Good Friday, Easter Vigil, Easter, Ordinary Time

   Review: We Celebrate Our Catholic Faith 40

PART THREE: We Live Our Catholic Faith

17. **True Happiness** 42
   Beatitude, Sin, Original Sin
18. **The Beatitudes** 44
   Beatitudes
19. **The Ten Commandments** 46
   Ten Commandments
20. **Conscience and Sin** 48
   Conscience, Sin, Mortal Sin, Venial Sin
21. **The Works of Mercy** 50
   Spiritual Works of Mercy, Corporal Works of Mercy
22. **Grace and Virtues** 52
   Sanctifying Grace, Actual Grace, Theological Virtues,
   Moral Virtues
23. **Thy Kingdom Come** 54
   Kingdom of God

   Review: We Live Our Catholic Faith 56

PART FOUR: We Pray

24. **Five Forms of Prayer** 58
   Prayer of Blessing and Adoration, Prayer of Petition, Prayer
   of Intercession, Prayer of Thanksgiving, Prayer of Praise
25. **Our Tradition of Prayer** 60
   Praying to the Father, the Son, the Holy Spirit;
   Praying to Mary and the Saints
26. **The Lord's Prayer** 62

   Review: We Pray 64

Treasury of Catholic Prayers and Practices 65

Faith Vocabulary 76

Part One
We Believe

How does the Church pass on the teachings of the apostles?

Read part one to learn more about the Sacred Tradition of the Catholic Church.

1
The Gift of Faith

Faith is a gift from God. Faith is God's invitation to trust and believe in him. It is also our response to that invitation.

At Mass we join with our parish community and profess our faith. We pray the Nicene Creed aloud. We begin,
> We believe in one God,
>> the Father, the Almighty,
>> maker of heaven and earth,
>> of all that is, seen and unseen.

What do we mean when we say that we believe in God?

To believe in someone means to have faith in or to put our trust in someone. We can also believe something because of the trustworthiness and truthfulness of the person who shares it with us. We believe in and trust God. We believe what God has revealed, or made known, to us. God is truthful and trustworthy beyond any doubt.

This is our Catholic faith. Faith is a gift from God. God is always trustworthy and always truthful and always good.

Our Catholic Tradition

Creeds
Creeds are also called professions of faith and symbols of faith. The Apostles' Creed and the Nicene Creed are two major creeds of Catholic Christians.

Placing Trust in God

Abram, whose name God later changed to Abraham, placed his trust in God. Read this Scripture passage about God's invitation to Abram. Use words or pictures to explain Abram's faith and trust in God.

God's Call to Abram

The LORD said to Abram, "Go from your country and your kindred and your father's house to the land that I will show you. I will make of you a great nation. . . ."

Abram went, as the LORD had told him . . . to the land of Canaan.

When they had come to the land of Canaan . . . the LORD appeared to Abram, and said, "To your offspring I will give this land." So he built there an altar to the LORD.

GENESIS 12:1–2, 4–5, 7

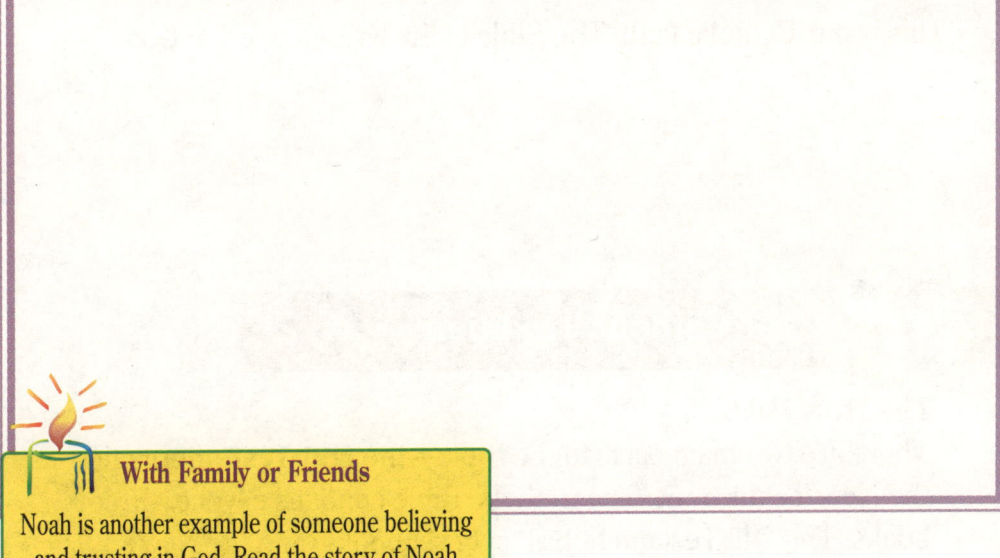

With Family or Friends

Noah is another example of someone believing and trusting in God. Read the story of Noah in Genesis 6:9–22, 7:1–24, and 8:1–19. Share this story with younger children.

2
Sacred Scripture

People can come to know God because God has revealed himself, or made himself known, to us.

In the **Sacred Scriptures,** or the **Bible,** we can come to know what God has revealed to us. The word *scripture* means "writing" and the word *bible* means "book." The Sacred Scripture is the written word of God. It shares with us what God's people came to know and believe about God.

Important truths that God shares with us about himself in the Bible are:
> God is one. There is only one true God.
> God is a mystery of three Persons—
> > Father, Son, and Holy Spirit.
>
> God is Truth and Love.
> God is Creator.
> God is Almighty and All-knowing.
> God is Holy and All-good.
> God is always Trustworthy, Merciful, and Forgiving.

This is our Catholic faith. The Bible is the written word of God.

Our Catholic Tradition

The Holy Bible
There are two main parts to the Bible—the **Old Testament** and the **New Testament.** The Catholic Bible contains seventy-three books. The Old Testament has forty-six books, and the New Testament has twenty-seven books. The most important writings in the New Testament are the four **Gospels.**

Understanding Sacred Scriptures

In the Bible we can come to know what God has revealed to us. Using the code below, discover two messages from the Bible.

A	B	C	D	E	F	G	H	I	J	K	L	M
1	2	3	4	5	6	7	8	9	10	11	12	13

N	O	P	Q	R	S	T	U	V	W	X	Y	Z
14	15	16	17	18	19	20	21	22	23	24	25	26

Message 1:

G O D   L O V E S   A   C H E E R F U L
7 15 4   12 15 22 5 19   1   3 8 5 5 18 6 21 12

G I V E R
7 9 22 5 18   **2 Corinthians 9:7**

Message 2:

Jesus said, " I A M W I T H Y O U
              9 1 13 23 9 20 8 25 15 21

A L W A Y S."
1 12 23 1 25 19   **Matthew 28:20**

With Family or Friends

Find a favorite Bible verse. Put the Bible verse into code by matching numbers and letters. Have someone try to figure out the code.

3
Sacred Tradition

God is revealed to us through **Sacred Tradition.** We give the name *sacred tradition* to the teachings and preaching of the **apostles**. The word *tradition* comes from a Latin word that means "to pass on." The apostles and the early church community passed on to us what God made known to us through Jesus Christ.

Jesus said,
> "I will send [the Spirit] to you. . . . When the Spirit . . . comes, he will guide you into all the truth." JOHN 16:7, 13

The Holy Spirit is our Teacher. The Holy Spirit helps and guides the whole community of the Church.

The Church is also our Teacher. The Church's teaching authority to teach what God has revealed is called the **magisterium.** The pope with all the bishops officially teach the true meaning of what God has revealed. The word *magisterium* comes from a word that means "teacher."

This is our Catholic faith. We believe that the Church teaches what God has revealed.

Our Catholic Tradition

Ecumenical Councils of the Church
Ecumenical councils are official gatherings of the pope, the bishops, and other church leaders. There have been twenty-one ecumenical councils. The Second Vatican Council was the last council. It began in 1962 under the leadership of Pope John XXIII and ended in 1965 under the leadership of Pope Paul VI.

Passing On Traditions

The Church is our Teacher. Fill in the missing words below by rereading the text on page 10. Decode the message by matching the numbers to the appropriate letters.

__ __ __ is revealed to us through Sacred Tradition.
7 15 4

The word *tradition* comes from a Latin word that means

"__ __ __ __ __ __ __ __." The __ __ __ __ __ __ has passed on the
 20 15 16 1 19 19 15 14   3 8 21 18 3 8

teaching and preaching of the __ __ __ __ __ __ __ __ to us. The __ __ __ __
                               1 16 15 19 20 12 5 19   8 15 12 25

__ __ __ __ __ __ helps us grow in our understanding of God.
19 16 9 18 9 20

__ __ __ __ __ __ __ __
 3 1 20 8 15 12 9 3 19

__ __ __ __ __
20 18 21 19 20

__ __ __ __ __ __ __ __ __ __ __ __ __ __ .
19 1 3 18 5 4   20 18 1 4 9 20 9 15 14

With Family or Friends

There are many teachers in your life who pass on the truths of our Catholic faith. Honor one of those teachers. Write a thank-you note to him or her.

4
The Mystery of the Holy Trinity

We name the mystery of God the **Holy Trinity.** This is the central belief of our Catholic faith. This is something we could never have known about God unless he revealed it.

God revealed to the Israelites that there is only one God.
> Hear, O Israel:
> The LORD is our God, the LORD alone. DEUTERONOMY 6:4

Jesus Christ revealed to us that there is one God, who is Father, Son, and Holy Spirit. Jesus prayed to God the Father. Jesus promised the disciples that he and the Father would send them the Holy Spirit.

Before he returned to the Father, Jesus said to his disciples,
> "Go therefore and make disciples of all nations,
> baptizing them in the name of the Father
> and of the Son and of the Holy Spirit." MATTHEW 28:19

This is our Catholic faith. We believe in the Holy Trinity. We believe that there are three Persons in the mystery of one God—God the Father, God the Son, and God the Holy Spirit.

Our Catholic Tradition

Blessings
We bless ourselves, our homes, statues, and other things that remind us of God. We bless them in the name of the Holy Trinity. We bless them, saying, "In the name of the Father, and of the Son, and of the Holy Spirit."

Praying Our Beliefs

The Apostles' Creed is a brief summary of the Church's beliefs. Using the words in the box, fill in the words to the Apostles' Creed.

| Son | forgiveness | died | Holy Spirit | ascended | born |
| creator | rose | suffered | everlasting | catholic | believe |

The Apostles' Creed

I _____ in God,
the Father almighty,

_____ of heaven and earth.

I believe in Jesus Christ,

his only _____ , our Lord.

He was conceived by the power
of the Holy Spirit and

_____ of the Virgin Mary.

He _____ under
Pontius Pilate, was crucified,

_____ , and was buried.
He descended into hell.

On the third day he _____ again.

He _____ into heaven
and is seated at the right hand
of the Father.
He will come again to judge
the living and the dead.

I believe in the _____ ,

the holy _____ Church,
the communion of saints,

the _____ of sins,
the resurrection of the body,

and the life _____ .

Amen.

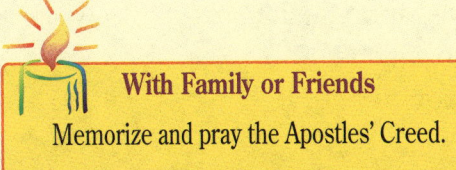

With Family or Friends
Memorize and pray the Apostles' Creed.

5
God the Father, Creator

God is the Creator of everything that is good. God created everything out of nothing. At Mass we profess our faith in God the Creator in the Nicene Creed. We say,

> We believe in one God,
> the Father, the Almighty,
> maker of heaven and earth,
> of all that is, seen and unseen.

God shares this truth about creation with us. In the very first sentence of the Bible, we read,

> In the beginning . . . God created the heavens and the earth. GENESIS 1:1

We believe that God created humans in his own image. God created us to share in his own goodness, love, and wisdom. Every person is an image of God. In the Bible story of creation, we read,

> Then God said,
> "Let us make humankind in our image,
> according to our likeness." GENESIS 1:26

This is our Catholic faith. We believe that God created the world out of love. Every person is created in the image of God.

Our Catholic Tradition

Divine Providence
God always cares for us out of his love for us. Jesus showed us this truth about God in the way he treated people. We call this **Divine Providence.**

Discovering Who God Is

The Apostles' Creed and the Nicene Creed tell what we believe about God. A coat of arms has symbols or words to tell about a person or family. Design a coat of arms for God.

With Family or Friends

Each bishop has a motto and a coat of arms. Write to your bishop to find out his motto and what his coat of arms looks like and means.

6
Jesus Christ, Our Lord and Savior

The name **Jesus** and the titles **Christ, Lord,** and **Savior** tell what we Catholics believe about Jesus.

Jesus is a Hebrew name that means "God saves." We believe that Jesus is our Savior. The angel appeared to Joseph and said,
> "[Mary] will bear a son, and you are to name him Jesus, for he will save his people from their sins." MATTHEW 1:21

Christ comes from the Hebrew word *messiah,* a word that means "anointed to do a special work for God." God promised to send the Messiah to save God's people. We believe that Jesus is the Christ, the Messiah. The Gospel of Mark tells us that Peter said to Jesus,
> "You are the Messiah." MARK 8:29

Lord is a very special title in the Bible. It is a title usually given only to God. After Jesus died and rose from the dead, Thomas the Apostle said to the risen Jesus,
> "My Lord and my God!" JOHN 20:28

This is our Catholic faith. We believe in the **incarnation** of the Son of God. The word *incarnation* means "becoming flesh." Jesus is truly God and truly man.

Our Catholic Tradition

Paschal Mystery
The death, resurrection, and ascension of Jesus Christ is called the **Paschal mystery.**

Discovering Who Jesus Is

Jesus is truly God and truly man. Solve the crossword puzzle. Each clue tells something about Jesus.

Across

2. _____ is the person to whom the angel appeared and said Mary would bear a son.
4. _____ is the Hebrew word that means "anointed to do a special work for God."
5. A very special title in the Bible given only to God is _____.
6. Jesus is the Son of _____.
7. Jesus is our _____ because he saves us from sin.

Down

1. *Incarnation* means "becoming _____."
2. A Hebrew name that means "God saves" is _____.
3. _____ comes from the Hebrew word *messiah*.
4. The mother of Jesus is _____.

With Family or Friends

Make up a game that helps people understand Jesus. Write your clues on one side of a card. Write your answers on the other side.

7
The Gift of the Holy Spirit

Jesus promised that he, the Father, and the Holy Spirit would always be with us. Jesus said,

> "Those who love me will keep my word, and my Father will love them, and we will come to them and make our home with them. . . . The Holy Spirit, whom the Father will send in my name, will teach you everything, and remind you of all that I have said to you." JOHN 14:23, 26

The New Testament tells us that Jesus kept his promise. The Holy Spirit did come as Helper and Teacher. On the Jewish feast of Pentecost, Jesus' followers were sitting together in a house. Suddenly they heard a strong wind blowing through the house. They saw tongues of fire over each one of them. And "all of them were filled with the Holy Spirit." BASED ON ACTS OF THE APOSTLES 2:2–4

Christians celebrate Pentecost as the birthday of the Church. On that day the apostles and other disciples began to preach and baptize as Jesus had told them. Thousands of people from many different countries became followers of Jesus on that day.

This is our Catholic faith. We believe that the Holy Spirit is always present with the Church as our Helper and Teacher.

Our Catholic Tradition

Easter-Ascension-Pentecost
We celebrate Jesus' Resurrection from the dead on Easter. We celebrate Jesus' return to his Father in heaven forty days after Easter, on the feast of the Ascension. We celebrate the coming of the Holy Spirit upon the disciples fifty days after Easter, on the feast of Pentecost.

Beginning the Church

Pentecost is the birthday of the Church. It is the day the Holy Spirit came upon the disciples. Add words to the frames below to show what the followers of Jesus might have said to one another on Pentecost.

With Family or Friends

We spread our Catholic faith through our words and actions. Illustrate with words or pictures how you can share your faith with others.

8
The Marks of the Church

We believe the Church has four **marks,** or four essential qualities. At Mass in the Nicene Creed we pray,

> We believe in one holy catholic
> and apostolic Church.

The Church Jesus founded is *one* Church. The Church is the Body of Christ. All members of the Church belong to Christ.

The Church is *holy.* The Church is the temple of the Holy Spirit, the holy People of God.

The Church is *catholic.* The word *catholic* means "universal." We believe that Jesus is the Savior of all people. God calls all people to belong to Christ.

The Church is *apostolic.* The word *apostolic* means "connected to the apostles." We believe that the Church today is the same Church that Jesus founded. With the help of the Holy Spirit, the Church today continues the work that Jesus gave the apostles.

This is our Catholic faith. The Church that Jesus founded is one, holy, catholic, and apostolic.

Our Catholic Tradition

Names of the Apostles
The apostles Jesus chose were Peter, John, James, Andrew, Matthew, Philip, Bartholomew, Thomas, James, Thaddeus, Simon, and Judas. After the resurrection and ascension of Jesus, Matthias, Paul, and Barnabas were named apostles.

Discovering What the New Testament Says about the Church

Jesus kept his promise in the New Testament. Read and think about these passages from the New Testament. Write the mark of the Church that each passage helps you understand.

Jesus prayed,

"[Father], may [they] become completely one, so that the world may know that you have sent me." JOHN 17:23

✓ _____

Saint Paul wrote,

Do you not know that you are God's temple and that God's Spirit dwells in you? 1 CORINTHIANS 3:16

✓ _____

Jesus gave his disciples this mission:

"Go therefore and make disciples of all nations, baptizing them in the name of the Father and of the Son and of the Holy Spirit." MATTHEW 28:19

✓ _____

Jesus said,

"And I tell you, you are Peter, and on this rock [the name *Peter* means "rock"] I will build my church." MATTHEW 16:18

✓ _____

With Family or Friends

Learn the names of the apostles. Choose one and learn more about the life and work of that apostle.

9
The People of God

The Church is the new **People of God**. At Baptism every member of the Church is called by God to work together. Laypeople, religious brothers and sisters, and ordained ministers are called by Baptism to live a holy life. We all are to use our gifts to continue the work of Jesus.

The **pope** and other **bishops** are successors of the apostles. The pope is the bishop of Rome and the successor of Saint Peter. He is the leader of the whole Catholic Church. The pope and the bishops teach the faith, lead the faithful in worshiping God, and guide us. Bishops are assisted in their work by **priests** and **deacons.** We call the leaders of the Church the **hierarchy.**

Members of the Church who are not ordained are called the **laity,** or **laypeople.** Laypeople use their talents to bring the Gospel to their families, the places where they work, and their communities. Laypeople work closely with bishops and priests to serve the Church.

Some men and women of the Church receive a special call from God to be a religious priest, brother, or sister. They live the **consecrated life.** They promise, or vow, to live lives of poverty, chastity, and obedience.

This is our Catholic faith. The People of God have the responsibility to continue the work of Jesus Christ and to live a holy life.

Our Catholic Tradition

Saint Francis Xavier
Francis was a member of the Society of Jesus and lived the consecrated life. He lived the Gospel as a missionary to the people of India. Saint Francis is the patron of foreign missions. We celebrate his feast day on December 3.

Naming the People of God

Every member of the Church is called by baptism to live a holy life and continue the work of Jesus. Name these members of the Church.

The _____ is the successor of Saint Peter, bishop of Rome, and leader of the Church.

_____ live a consecrated life and take vows of poverty, chastity, and obedience.

_____ are nonordained members of the Church who continue the work of Jesus Christ in their families, in their workplaces, and in their communities.

_____ are successors of the apostles, and teachers of the faith.

With Family or Friends

Interview members of your family to find out how they live as people of God.

10
Mary, the Mother of God

From the first moment of her existence, Mary was free from all sin—original sin and personal sin. We call this the **Immaculate Conception of Mary.**

The **Virgin Mary** plays a special role in God's plan of salvation. An angel announced to her that God chose her to be the mother of the Son of God.

Mary responded "yes" to become the mother of God's Son, Jesus. Throughout her life Mary was with Jesus. The Holy Family worked and prayed together in Nazareth. They traveled together to the Temple in Jerusalem to celebrate Jewish feasts.

Mary was present in Cana when Jesus helped the newly married couple. She was with Jesus when he suffered and died. The Gospel of John tells us she was at the foot of the cross on Calvary.

After Jesus rose from the dead, she was with the disciples in Jerusalem when the Holy Spirit came upon them.

At the end of her life, Mary was taken into heaven body and soul. We call this the **Assumption of Mary.** She lives with God and shares in the glory of her risen Son, Jesus. She is the Queen of Heaven and Earth.

This is our Catholic faith. We believe that the Blessed Virgin Mary is the Mother of God.

Our Catholic Tradition

Miraculous Medal
Medals are sacramentals. We Catholics wear medals to remind us of our faith. We wear the Miraculous Medal in honor of the Immaculate Conception of Mary.

Telling the Story of Mary's Life

The Blessed Virgin Mary has a special role in God's plan of salvation. Using this Table of Contents, write the remaining chapter titles that will tell Mary's story.

Table of Contents

Chapter 1 Full of Grace	1
Chapter 2	10
Chapter 3	20
Chapter 4	30
Chapter 5	40
Chapter 6	50
Chapter 7	60
Chapter 8 Queen of Heaven and Earth	70

With Family or Friends

Draw an illustration for one of your chapters. Using your illustration, tell this chapter of Mary's life to a friend.

REVIEW OF PART ONE
We Believe

Match the faith terms with the descriptions in the right column.

1. _____ Pentecost
2. _____ Immaculate Conception
3. _____ Messiah
4. _____ Nicene Creed
5. _____ Incarnation
6. _____ laity
7. _____ catholic
8. _____ faith
9. _____ Sacred Scripture
10. _____ Sacred Tradition

a. A profession of faith said at Mass

b. Universal, welcoming all people

c. Mary, the Mother of God, from the moment of her existence was full of grace

d. A gift from God to trust and believe in God

e. The birthday of the Church

f. "Becoming flesh"—Jesus is truly God and truly man

g. The written word of God

h. Baptized people who are not members of the hierarchy

i. The teaching and preaching passed on to us by the apostles and the early Church

j. A word that means "anointed to do special work for God"

PART TWO
We Celebrate Our Catholic Faith

How do we celebrate our faith?

Read part two to learn about the liturgy and the seven sacraments.

11
The Liturgy and the Sacraments

When we celebrate the **liturgy,** we take part in the work of God. The word *liturgy* means "work of the people." The liturgy of the Church is the work of the whole Church.

The celebration of the seven **sacraments** is at the center of the Church's liturgy and prayer. Jesus instituted, or gave us, the sacraments. Christ is present and continues his work of salvation through the sacraments. The sacraments make us sharers in the life of God.

These are the seven sacraments:

* The **Sacraments of Christian Initiation,** which are Baptism, Confirmation, and Eucharist;
* The **Sacraments of Healing,** which are Penance and Anointing of the Sick;
* The **Sacraments at the Service of Communion,** which are Holy Orders and Matrimony.

Celebrating the seven sacraments makes our relationship with the Holy Trinity—God the Father, the Son, and the Holy Spirit—and the Church stronger. The Church with the help of the Holy Spirit joins with Christ to give thanks and praise to the Father in prayer.

This is our Catholic faith. Celebrating the sacraments joins us more closely with God and with the People of God, the Church. The sacraments allow us to share in the life and work of God.

Our Catholic Tradition

Statues and Other Sacramentals
Statues, stained-glass windows, holy water, medals, and blessings are some of the sacramentals given to us by the Church. Sacramentals help us to be more aware of God's presence with us and deepen our faith in God.

Finding Sacrament Words

Jesus instituted, or gave us, the sacraments. Using key words on page 28, fill in this acrostic puzzle. The letter "m" has been done as an example.

```
          s
          a
          c
          r
          a
Confirmation
          e
          n
          t
```

With Family or Friends

Using the words you selected, write a poem or song about the sacraments.

12
Sacraments of Initiation

The three **Sacraments of Christian Initiation** are Baptism, Confirmation, and Eucharist. These three sacraments are the foundation of our Christian life.

Baptism is the first sacrament we celebrate. Baptism is the beginning of a new life. In Baptism, original sin and all the sins we have committed are forgiven. We are welcomed into of the Body of Christ, the Church. We receive the Holy Spirit. We are called to live a holy life and continue the work of Christ.

We can be baptized only once. Baptism leaves a character, or sign, on our soul. It marks us forever as belonging to Christ.

Confirmation is the second Sacrament of Initiation. The celebration of Confirmation completes our Baptism. We receive the gift of the Holy Spirit and the **grace** to live as Christians.

We can be confirmed only once. Confirmation, too, leaves a character, or mark, on our soul. It marks us forever as belonging to Christ.

This is our Catholic faith. The Sacraments of Initiation celebrate our becoming members of the Church. In Baptism we become children of God, members of the Catholic Church. The Holy Spirit comes to us in a special way and we share in God's life.

Our Catholic Tradition

The Church's Oils
The Church uses three special oils blessed by the bishop in the celebration of the sacraments. Chrism is used in Baptism, Confirmation, and Holy Orders. Oil of the sick is used in Anointing of the Sick. Oil of catechumens is used in Baptism.

Naming the Sacraments

The Sacraments of Initiation are the foundation of our Christian life. Write the names of the sacraments or other words about the sacraments that match the clues.

This is a blessed oil. It is used in
Baptism and Confirmation. _____

This is a Sacrament of Initiation.
This is the first sacrament we celebrate. _____

This is a Sacrament of Initiation.
This sacrament completes our Baptism. _____

This is a Sacrament of Initiation.
It is the third Sacrament of Initiation. _____

With Family or Friends
Learn how your parish celebrates welcoming new members into the Church. Share what you learn with others.

13
The Mass

The celebration of the sacrament of the **Eucharist** completes our initiation into the Body of Christ, the Church. Participating in the Eucharist unites us most fully with the Holy Trinity—God the Father, the Son, and the Holy Spirit—and with one another. We join with Christ and the community of believers in giving thanks and praise to God the Father.

The Eucharist is also called the **Holy Sacrifice of the Mass.** The celebration of the Mass has two main parts, the **Liturgy of the Word** and the **Liturgy of the Eucharist.** The Mass always includes:

- proclaiming the word of God;
- praising and thanking God the Father for God's gifts, especially the gift of Jesus, the Son of God;
- the consecration of the bread and wine; and
- sharing in the Lord's Body and Blood in Holy Communion.

The Eucharist is the memorial of Christ's Passover. It is thanksgiving and praise to God the Father. It is the sacrificial memorial of Christ and his Body. It is the presence of Christ by the power of his word and of his spirit.

This is our Catholic faith. We believe that the bread and wine at Mass truly and really become the Body and Blood of Christ. The word the Church uses to name this belief is **transubstantiation.**

Our Catholic Tradition

Blessed Sacrament

The **Blessed Sacrament** is the consecrated Body and Blood of Jesus. The lighted sanctuary lamp tells us that after Mass the Blessed Sacrament is reserved, or kept, in the tabernacle. Christ is truly and really present there.

Celebrating the Eucharist

The Eucharist celebrates the memorial of Christ's Passover. Using the code, discover an important truth Catholics believe about the Holy Sacrifice of the Mass.

A	B	C	D	E	F	G	H	I	J	K	L	M
1	2	3	4	5	6	7	8	9	10	11	12	13

N	O	P	Q	R	S	T	U	V	W	X	Y	Z
14	15	16	17	18	19	20	21	22	23	24	25	26

T H E   B R E A D   A N D   W I N E
20 8 5   2 18 5 1 4   1 14 4   23 9 14 5

A T   M A S S   B E C O M E   T H E
1 20   13 1 19 19   2 5 3 15 13 5   20 8 5

B O D Y   A N D   B L O O D   O F
2 15 4 25   1 14 4   2 12 15 15 4   15 6

C H R I S T   J E S U S   I S
3 8 18 9 19 20   10 5 19 21 19   9 19

T R U L Y   A N D   R E A L L Y
20 18 21 12 25   1 14 4   18 5 1 12 12 25

P R E S E N T   W I T H   U S .
16 18 5 19 5 14 20   23 9 20 8   21 19

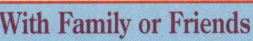

With Family or Friends
Look up and quietly read in your Bible the story about the Last Supper that can be found in Mark 14:12–26. Then choose people to play the parts of Jesus, the disciples, and the narrator. Read the story aloud.

14
Sacraments of Healing

Penance and Anointing of the Sick are called the **Sacraments of Healing.** They make Jesus' work of forgiveness and healing present among us.

The sacrament of **Penance** celebrates that God is with us to forgive us when we sin. This sacrament is also called the sacrament of Reconciliation. The celebration of the sacrament of Penance includes:

- **Contrition,** or repentance. We are truly sorry for our sins and we promise to try not to sin again.
- **Confession.** We tell our sins to the priest or bishop.
- **Penance,** or satisfaction for our sins. We are trying to make up for sins.
- **Absolution.** God forgives us through the words and actions of the priest.

Jesus helped many people who were seriously ill. The sacrament of **Anointing of the Sick** strengthens our faith when we are seriously sick or dying. In Anointing of the Sick the priest anoints our hands and forehead with the **oil of the sick.**

This is our Catholic faith. Jesus gave us the sacraments of Penance and Anointing of the Sick. These sacraments continue Jesus' work of forgiveness and healing in our lives.

Our Catholic Tradition

Saint Mary Magdalene
The Gospels tell us Jesus forgave Mary Magdalene her sins. She was also the first disciple to whom Jesus appeared after his resurrection. Mary Magdalene is the patron of friendships. We celebrate her feast day on July 22.

Writing about Healing

The Sacraments of Healing make Jesus' work of forgiveness and healing present among us. Look at these pictures. Write the words and thoughts you have about healing.

With Family or Friends
Mother Teresa of Calcutta is a model of healing. Interview your family, friends, or a member of your parish. Find out about other people who are healers.

15
Sacraments at the Service of Communion

Some members of the Church have a special vocation, or calling, to serve the whole church community. The Church celebrates this special vocation in the two **Sacraments at the Service of Communion.** These are Holy Orders and Matrimony.

In the sacrament of **Holy Orders,** bishops, priests, and deacons are ordained to serve the whole Church. In this sacrament a bishop lays his hands on the man who is to be ordained and says a special prayer. This shows that those ordained receive a special grace of the Holy Spirit to serve the Church.

At the ordination of a bishop, the ordaining bishop gives the bishop a pastoral staff, saying,
> Take this staff as a sign of your pastoral office:
> keep watch over the whole flock
> in which the Holy Spirit has appointed you
> the shepherd of the Church of God.

The sacrament of **Matrimony** celebrates that a man and woman are a sign of Christ's love for us. In the special blessing of the couple, the priest prays,
> Father, . . .
> Keep them faithful in marriage
> and let them be living examples of Christian life.

In this sacrament a baptized man and woman freely promise to enter into a lifelong marriage with each other. A married man and woman are called by God to form a family. They receive a special grace from the Holy Spirit. This grace helps them faithfully love and honor each other throughout their lives.

This is our Catholic faith. Jesus gave us the sacraments of Holy Orders and Matrimony. They celebrate God's calling of a bishop, priest, deacon, and a husband and wife to serve the whole Church.

Serving Others

Bishops, priests, deacons, and married couples have the vocation to serve the whole Church. Find words in the puzzle about the Sacraments at the Service of Communion. Tell what the words mean to you.

vocation Holy Orders Matrimony bishop priest deacon
sacrament service apostles pope ordained grace

```
P A S A C R A M E N T
O R D A I N E D U W M
P G Q X P H R I N C A
E R R M R O V B E S P
M A T R I M O N Y E O
E C H A E O C Z S R S
S E P C S N A A E V T
R S A S T L T T R I L
F T G F G D I D M C E
B Z B I S H O P I E S
Y D E A C O N E C M E
H O L Y O R D E R S B
```

With Family or Friends

Interview a priest, a bishop, a deacon, or a married couple to find out the different ways they serve the Church. After the interview write a job description.

16
The Liturgical Year

We celebrate the liturgy throughout the year. We call this year of celebration the Church's **liturgical year.**

The four weeks of **Advent** begin the liturgical year. During Advent we prepare for Christmas. We thank God for always being with us. We remember the promise that Christ will come again in glory at the end of time.

The **Christmas** season begins on Christmas Eve. It lasts for three weeks until the celebration of the Baptism of the Lord. We praise and thank God for the birth of Jesus, the Savior of the whole world.

The forty days of **Lent** prepare us for Easter. During Lent we renew our efforts to live our baptismal promises. We give alms, or help others. We fast and abstain, or "give things up," to remember we are children of God. We pray more often.

Holy Thursday, Good Friday, and the celebration of the **Easter Vigil** are called the **Easter Triduum.** We celebrate and remember the last days of Jesus' life and his rising from the dead. **Easter** is a fifty-day season that celebrates Jesus' resurrection from the dead. We believe that we too will rise from the dead and live with Jesus forever.

Ordinary Time is the name we give to all the other weeks of the year.

This is our Catholic faith. Throughout the year we celebrate all that God has done for us in Christ.

Our Catholic Tradition

Blessing with Ashes
Ash Wednesday is the beginning of the season of Lent. On this day ashes made from burned palm branches are used to trace the sign of the cross on our foreheads. This reminds us that we are to live a holy life as Jesus taught us.

Following the Liturgical Year

We celebrate the liturgy throughout the year. In the wheel write one way we follow Jesus in each part of the liturgical year.

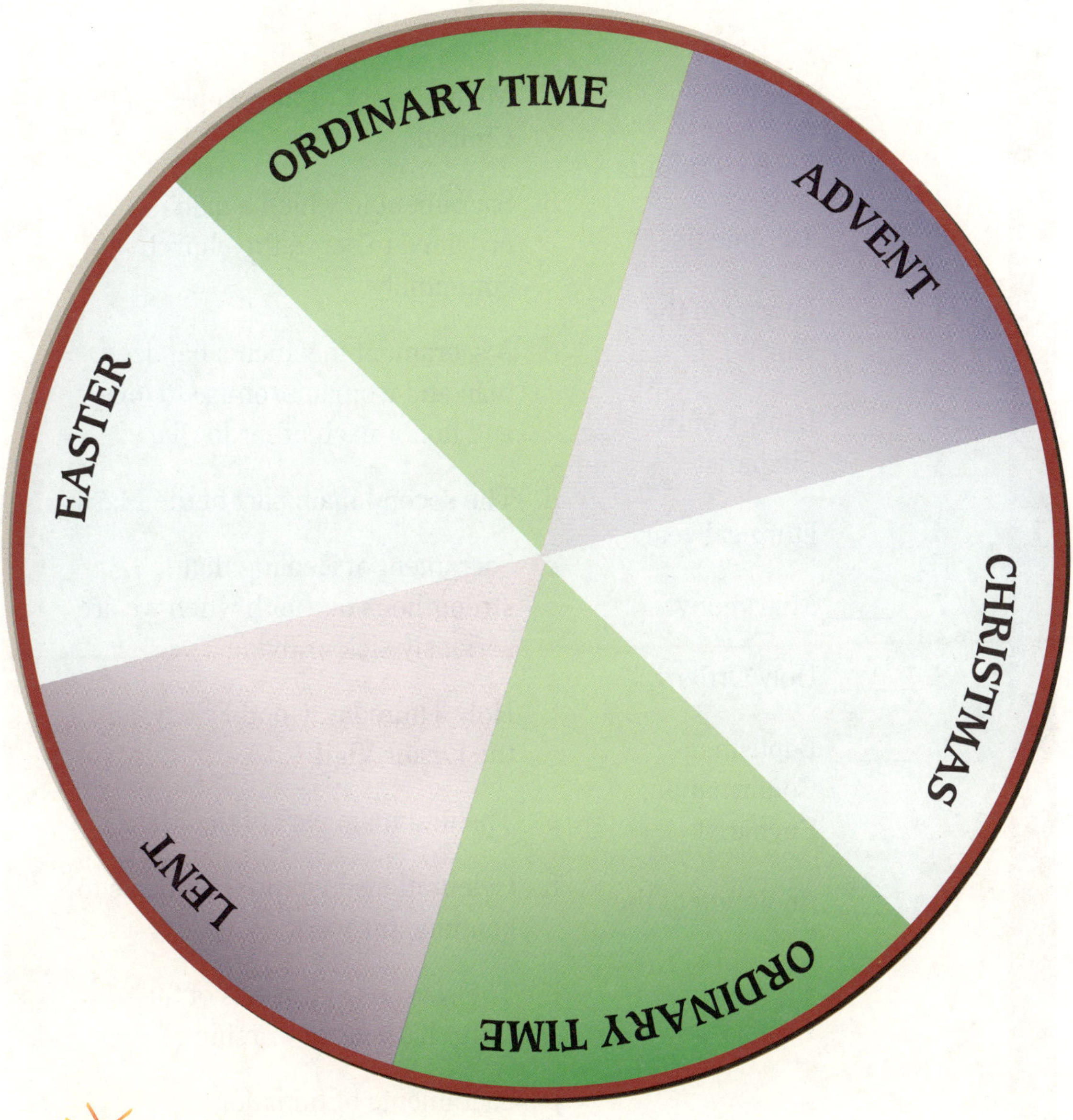

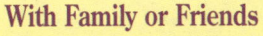

With Family or Friends

Research the colors the Church uses during each part of the liturgical year. Design a banner, using the appropriate color for one of the seasons.

Review of Part Two
We Celebrate Our Catholic Faith

Match the faith terms with the descriptions in the right column.

1. _____ liturgy
2. _____ Easter Triduum
3. _____ sacraments
4. _____ Liturgy of the Word
5. _____ Liturgy of the Eucharist
6. _____ liturgical year
7. _____ Matrimony
8. _____ Holy Orders
9. _____ Baptism, Confirmation, Eucharist
10. _____ Anointing of the Sick

a. Means "work of the people" of the Church
b. Sacrament in which a man is ordained to serve the church community
c. A sacrament in which a baptized man and woman promise to love and honor each other for life
d. The second main part of the Mass
e. Sacrament of Healing that strengthens our faith when we are seriously sick or dying
f. Holy Thursday, Good Friday, and the Easter Vigil
g. The first main part of the Mass
h. Celebrations instituted by Jesus to continue his work
i. The seasons and feasts of the Church's year of worship
j. Sacraments of Initiation

Part Three
We Live Our Catholic Faith

How do we live our Catholic faith?

Read part three to learn how the commandments and Beatitudes help us live as Catholics.

17
True Happiness

God calls us to share in his love and joy. This happiness, or **beatitude,** is God's free gift to us. We come to the happiness that God puts in our hearts by living in a certain way. True happiness calls us to make certain choices and to develop certain attitudes.

We do not come to this true happiness by simply being wealthy, famous, or popular. Having a lot of power or achieving great things in technology, science, or the arts is not happiness. True happiness comes from our trust and faith in God. True happiness comes from living our friendship with God.

When we purposely, or intentionally, do things to weaken or break that friendship, we **sin.** Sin is an offense against God and God's law. Sin contributes to our own unhappiness and the unhappiness of others. This truth is revealed to us in the Bible story of Adam and Eve, which teaches us about **original sin.**

This is our Catholic faith. God calls us to share in the life of joy and happiness of the Holy Trinity. Sin leads us away from that joy and happiness.

Our Catholic Tradition

Capital Sins
The Church names seven capital sins. They are called "capital" because they are the source for other sins as well. The seven capital sins are pride, avarice, envy, wrath, lust, gluttony, and sloth. When we choose to commit these sins, we are choosing a false happiness.

Sharing in God's Life and Joy

God shares his love and joy with us. We show people God's love when we care for them. Write how people in these photos are sharing God's love. In the box, show how you share God's love with someone else.

With Family or Friends

The saints showed people the meaning of true happiness. Research five saints. Create a saints book with the title "The Way to True Happiness."

18
The Beatitudes

Jesus taught us about the actions and attitudes that lead us to true happiness. We find this teaching of Jesus in the eight **Beatitudes**.

These are the Beatitudes:

"Blessed are the poor in spirit. . . .	The poor in spirit have faith in and trust God.
"Blessed are those who mourn. . . .	Those who mourn are sad when they see evil and try to help people who are hurt by evil.
"Blessed are the meek. . . .	The meek treat others kindly and respectfully.
"Blessed are those who hunger and thirst for righteousness. . . .	Those who hunger and thirst for righteousness work for justice. They want everyone to be treated fairly.
"Blessed are the merciful. . . .	The merciful reach out to and help others. They forgive others as God forgives them.
"Blessed are the pure in heart. . . .	The pure in heart keep God first in their lives.
"Blessed are the peacemakers. . . .	Peacemakers solve problems without harming anyone.
"Blessed are those who are persecuted for righteousness' sake. . . ." MATTHEW 5:3–10	Those persecuted for righteousness do what God wants, even when others laugh at them or threaten to harm them.

This is our Catholic faith. Jesus taught us the Beatitudes. They show us the way to the kingdom of heaven.

Understanding the Beatitudes

The Beatitudes show us the way to the kingdom of heaven. Write a Beatitude for each headline.

Community Meets to Solve Tensions

_____
_____
_____

Marchers Heckled at Peace Rally

_____
_____
_____
_____

Great Leader Dies, Many Attend Funeral

_____
_____
_____
_____

NEIGHBOR FORGIVES NEIGHBOR

_____
_____
_____
_____

Mother Teresa Honored at United Nations

_____
_____
_____

Family Adopts Homeless Person

_____
_____
_____

With Family or Friends

Make a collage, using other newspaper or magazine headlines that illustrate the Beatitudes.

19
The Ten Commandments

Jesus taught us that we are to live the **Ten Commandments.** The Ten Commandments are also called the Decalogue, which means "ten words."

The Ten Commandments are God's very own word to us. They make God's will known to us. They tell us what it means to belong to God. They teach us the basic rules that sum up the way we are to live as God's people. They tell us how we can live the **Great Commandment.**

> "You shall love the Lord your God with all your heart, and with all your soul, and with all your mind."
>
> MATTHEW 22:37

The first three commandments are about loving God. They tell us how we shall love the Lord our God with all our heart, with all our soul, and with all our mind. The next seven commandments are about loving other people and ourselves.

We have a serious responsibility to try to understand and live the Ten Commandments. We believe that the Holy Spirit helps us understand and live the Ten Commandments. The pope and the bishops and the church community teach us the meaning of the Ten Commandments. Our parents and other family members guide us in living the Ten Commandments each day.

This is our Catholic faith. The Ten Commandments are God's very own word to us. They show us how to live as God's people.

With Family or Friends

Find stories that illustrate people living the Great Commandment. Work with others to create a newspaper reporting these stories.

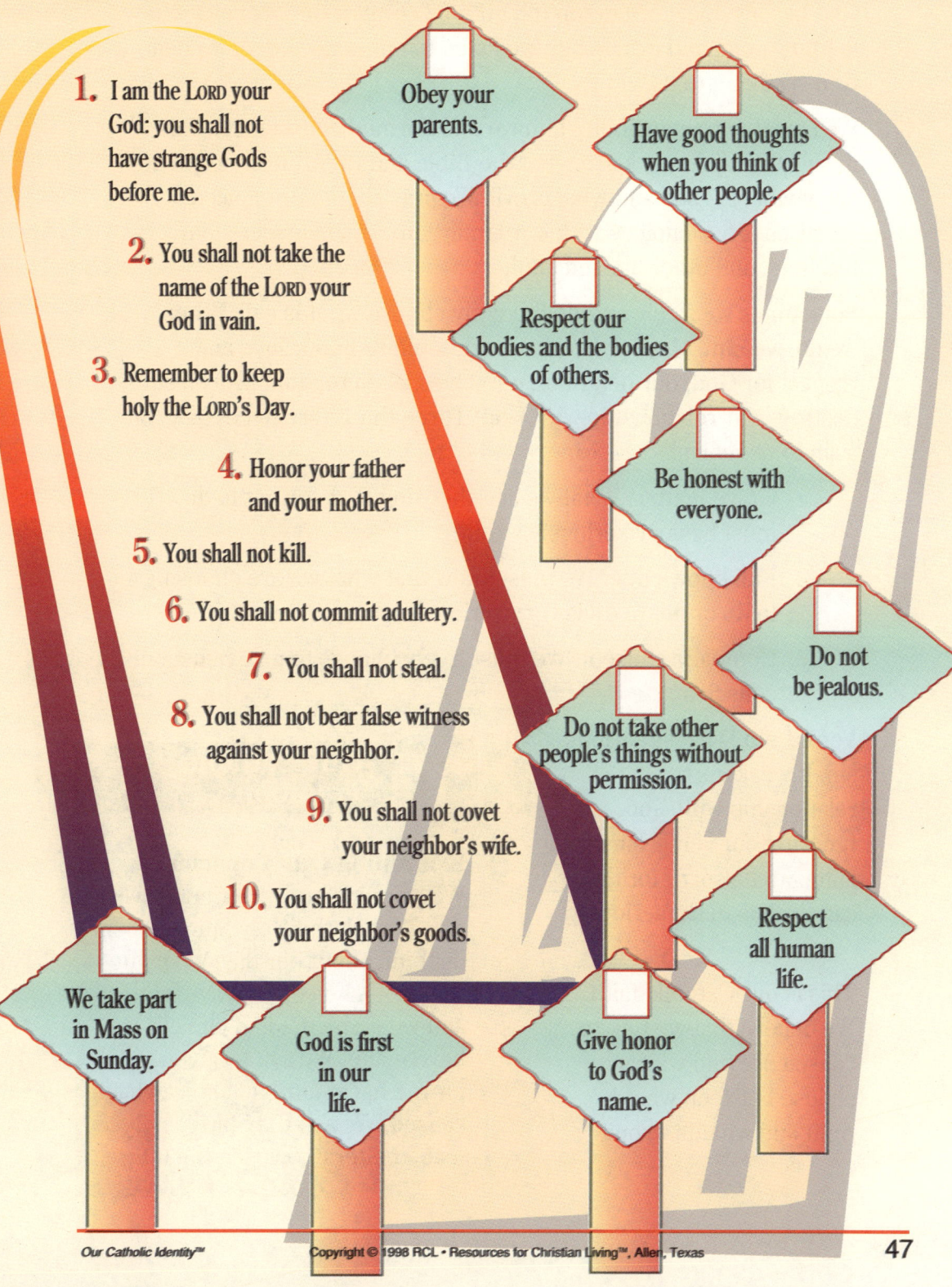

20
Conscience and Sin

God has given every person the gift of a **conscience.** It guides us to know good and evil. When we listen to our conscience, we hear God speaking to us.

We have the responsibility to have an informed conscience. This means that we must learn what the Bible and the Church teach us about what is good and what is evil. We pray about our choices. We discuss our choices with our family, our parish leaders, our teachers, and other trusted adults.

Sometimes we freely and deliberately choose what is evil. When we do, we **sin. Mortal sin** is a serious failure in our love and respect for God, our neighbor, ourselves, and creation. Mortal sin destroys our relationship with God. Three things are necessary for a sin to be mortal.

1. Grave matter: What we are choosing to do or not to do must be very seriously wrong.

2. Full knowledge: We must know that what we are choosing to do or not to do is very seriously wrong.

3. Complete consent: We must freely choose to go against our conscience.

Venial sin is a less serious sin. It weakens our relationship with God. Ignoring our venial sins or failing to be sorry for them can lead us to sin seriously.

This is our Catholic faith. We believe that we have a conscience and we can choose between what is right and what is wrong.

Our Catholic Tradition

Examining Our Conscience
We examine our conscience every day. We ask the Holy Spirit to help us think about our day. We name the good choices we have made and we name the bad choices we have made. We ask forgiveness for the harm our bad choices have caused. We ask the Spirit's help to make better choices in the future.

Making Choices

The Church's teaching and the Ten Commandments help us to have an informed conscience. Read the following moral dilemmas. Select one of the Ten Commandments listed on page 47 that each person in these stories could use to solve the dilemmas to live as a child of God.

All the kids in Paul's group are beginning to swear. Paul feels as if he has to swear in order to be part of the group. On what commandment should Paul reflect? _____

Linda and her friends think that it is cool to take inexpensive merchandise from the stores at the mall. On what commandment should Linda reflect? _____

Craig moves to a new school where he tells everyone that he and his family have traveled to several different countries. In fact, Craig has never left the state. On what commandment should Craig reflect? _____

With Family or Friends

Talk over with someone the steps for making a good decision. Put the steps into action.

21
The Works of Mercy

We Catholics believe that we find true happiness when we live the **works of mercy.** The word *mercy* comes from two Hebrew words meaning "being faithful out of love."

The works of mercy guide us in living the Gospel. The Church has named fourteen works of mercy. There are seven Spiritual Works of Mercy and seven Corporal Works of Mercy.

These are the **Spiritual Works of Mercy:**
- Help people who sin.
- Teach people who are ignorant.
- Give advice to people who have doubts.
- Comfort people who suffer.
- Be patient with other people.
- Forgive people who hurt you.
- Pray for people who are alive and for those who have died.

These are the **Corporal Works of Mercy:**
- Feed people who are hungry.
- Give drink to people who are thirsty.
- Clothe people who need clothes.
- Visit prisoners.
- Shelter people who are homeless.
- Visit people who are sick.
- Bury people who have died.

This is our Catholic faith. We believe and trust that by living the works of mercy we are doing what Jesus asked us to do: "This is my commandment, that you love one another as I have loved you."
JOHN 15:12

Describing a Work of Mercy

People are living the Gospel. Using the chart and the works of mercy on page 50, write a news report that shows people living a work of mercy.

Who	What	Where	When
you	help someone break the habit of taking other people's things	at the mall	last week
your family	brings food for an elderly person	in your neighborhood	on Saturday
your teacher	gives used books to a children's hospital	at a soccer game	during recess
your best friends	make friends with a new neighbor	at school	in the evening
your idea	*your idea*	*your idea*	*your idea*

News Report by _____

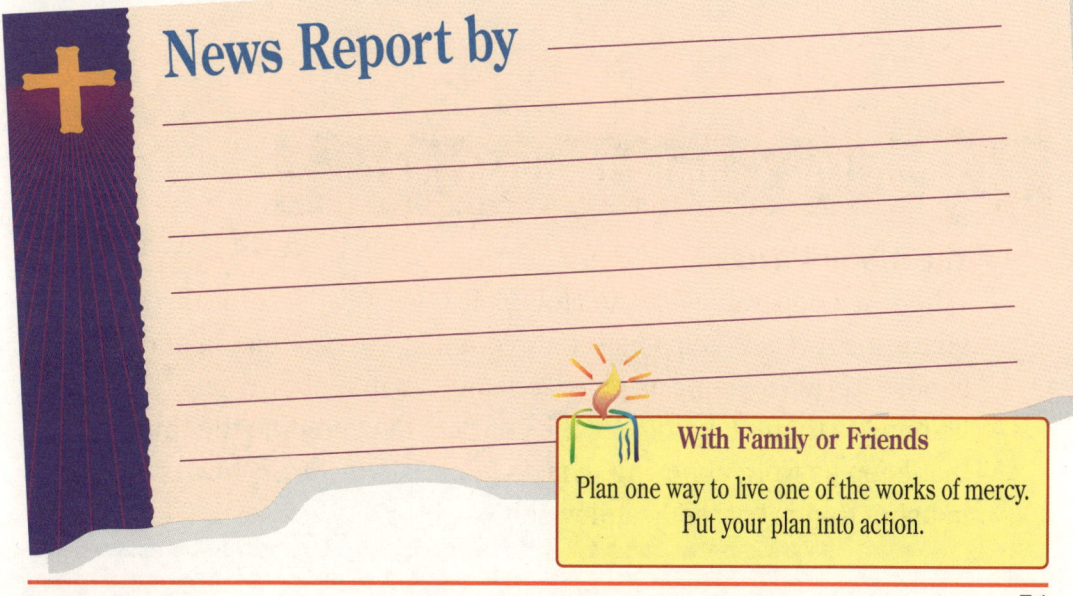

With Family or Friends

Plan one way to live one of the works of mercy. Put your plan into action.

22
Grace and Virtues

We believe God makes us sharers in the life of the Holy Trinity and helps us live as children of God. We call these gifts from God **grace.**

The three **theological virtues** are gifts from God. The word *virtue* means "a power or habit to do something." The three theological virtues are faith, hope, and charity (or love). Saint Paul teaches us,

> And now faith, hope, and love abide, these three; and the greatest of these is love. 1 CORINTHIANS 13:13

Faith is the virtue by which we believe in God and in all God has revealed to us.

Hope is the virtue by which we place our trust in God's promises.

Charity, or love, is the virtue by which we love God above all things and others as ourselves.

This is our Catholic faith. God shares his life and love with us. We call this **sanctifying grace.** God helps us live as children of God. We call this **actual grace.**

Our Catholic Tradition

The Moral Virtues
When we cooperate with the Holy Spirit, we develop **moral virtues.** *Prudence* helps us see the good in every situation and choose it. *Justice* helps us give God and our neighbor what belongs to them. *Fortitude* is the courage to overcome the things that keep us from choosing what is good. *Temperance* guides us in using things correctly and wisely.

Living Our Virtues

The virtues help us live as children of God. Complete the crossword puzzle about the virtues.

Across

2. This moral virtue strengthens us to overcome temptation.
5. This moral virtue enables us to see good in every situation.
6. This theological virtue helps us place our trust in God's promise of love.
7. This theological virtue helps us love God and neighbor.
9. This moral virtue enables us to give God and our neighbor what is due them.

Down

1. There are four of this kind of virtue.
2. This theological virtue helps us believe in God.
3. This moral virtue guides us in using created things wisely.
4. This can be both sanctifying and actual.
8. This describes the three Persons in one God.

With Family or Friends

Name a person you know who lives the virtues of faith, hope, and charity. Tell something about this person's life.

23
Thy Kingdom Come

In the Our Father we pray, "Thy kingdom come." Jesus announced the coming of God's kingdom.

> Now after John was arrested, Jesus came to Galilee, proclaiming the good news of God, and saying, "The time is fulfilled, and the kingdom of God has come near; repent, and believe in the good news." MARK 1:14–15

The Good News proclaimed by Jesus is that all people are invited to be part of God's kingdom. No one is excluded by God. The kingdom of God will be built by living the Gospel.

Treating one another with respect and sharing our talents and blessings with one another brings about the kingdom of God. Treating others with disrespect and keeping our talents and blessings to ourselves does not.

This is our Catholic faith. All people are invited into the kingdom of God that Jesus proclaimed. We join with Jesus to bring about the coming of God's kingdom.

Our Catholic Tradition

Saint Elizabeth of Hungary
Elizabeth was the daughter of the king of Hungary. She treated everyone with respect and love. After her husband died, Elizabeth used her wealth to care for the poor and the sick. Saint Elizabeth is the patron saint of hospitals and Catholic Charities. We celebrate her feast day on November 17.

Working for Others

We are called to build the kingdom of God. Read this Scripture passage to understand the importance of using your talents to build the kingdom of God. In the base of each light, write a talent you are using.

"You are the light of the world. A city built on a hill cannot be hid. No one after lighting a lamp puts it under the bushel basket, but on the lampstand, and it gives light to all in the house. In the same way, let your light shine before others, so that they may see your good works and give glory to your Father in heaven."

MATTHEW 5:14–16

With Family or Friends

Light up someone's day. Develop a plan to be kind to someone. Put your plan into action.

REVIEW OF PART THREE
We Live Our Catholic Faith

Match the faith terms with the descriptions in the right column.

1. _____ Great Commandment
2. _____ mortal sin
3. _____ conscience
4. _____ Ten Commandments
5. _____ Beatitudes
6. _____ Corporal Works of Mercy
7. _____ venial sin
8. _____ virtues
9. _____ sin
10. _____ grace

a. A guide inside us to do good and avoid evil

b. Actions that help us live the commandments

c. Our sharing in God's life

d. Choosing evil and acting against our conscience

e. Rules or laws that make God's will known to us. They are God's very own words.

f. A less serious failure in our love for God and neighbor

g. The actions and attitudes that lead us to true happiness

h. A serious failure in our love for God and neighbor

i. Powers or habits that help us live as children of God

j. The commandment that expresses our love for God, others, and ourselves

PART FOUR
We Pray

What are the different ways we pray?

Read part four to learn how to respond to God's invitation to prayer.

24
Five Forms of Prayer

Prayer is our talking and listening to God, who is always inviting us to share God's life and love. There are five basic forms of prayer.

In our prayer of blessing and adoration we acknowledge God to be our almighty Creator. We bless God, who is the source of everything that is good. At Mass we pray:
> Blessed are you, Lord, God of all creation . . .

In our prayer of petition we ask for God's forgiveness and for help in all our needs. Jesus taught us to pray,
> Give us this day our daily bread,
> and forgive us our trespasses . . .

In our prayer of intercession we pray that all people will be joined with Christ and come to know God's love for them. Jesus prayed,
> "As you, Father, are in me and I am in you,
> may they also be in us." JOHN 17:21

In our prayer of thanksgiving we join with Christ and thank God for everything, especially the gift of salvation. At Mass we pray,
> Father, all-powerful and ever-living God,
> we do well always and everywhere to give you thanks
> through Jesus Christ our Lord.

In our prayer of praise we acknowledge that God is God and that we are children of God. At Mass we pray,
> Father, you are holy indeed,
> and all creation rightly gives you praise.

This is our Catholic faith. We believe we can talk and listen to God in prayer.

Praying in Different Ways

Prayer is our talking and listening to God, who is always inviting us to share in God's life and love. List the five forms of prayer. Select two and create your prayers.

Forms of Prayers

With Family or Friends

Design a bookmark that has your favorite part of a prayer. Share it with a friend.

25
Our Tradition of Prayer

We begin our prayers in the name of the **Holy Trinity.** We pray,

> In the name of the Father, and of the Son,
> and of the Holy Spirit. Amen.

We pray to **God the Father,** our Creator. Jesus taught us to pray,

> Our Father who art in heaven,
> hallowed be thy name.

We pray to **God the Son,** our Lord and Savior Jesus Christ. We pray anywhere, anytime, everywhere and always by invoking, or calling upon, the holy name of Jesus. We pray,

> Praised be Jesus Christ.

We pray to **God the Holy Spirit,** the Giver of Life, who teaches us to pray. We pray,

> Come, Holy Spirit, fill the hearts of your faithful.
> And kindle in them the fire of your love.

We also pray to the **Blessed Virgin Mary,** the Holy Mother of God, and to the **saints.** The saints hear our prayers and bring them to the Father in the name of Jesus.

This is our Catholic faith. We pray to God the Father, God the Son, and God the Holy Spirit. We also pray to Mary and the other saints.

Our Catholic Tradition

Ways of Expressing our Prayers
We name several ways of expressing, or saying, our prayers. They are vocal prayer, meditation, contemplation, personal prayer, and communal prayer.

Praying

We can pray anywhere and anytime. To solve the puzzle, fill in the correct words in the pyramid of eleven words. Notice that each word has the same number of letters as the number by its side. To find the eleven words, complete the eleven statements. Then use the shaded letters in the pyramid to answer the question.

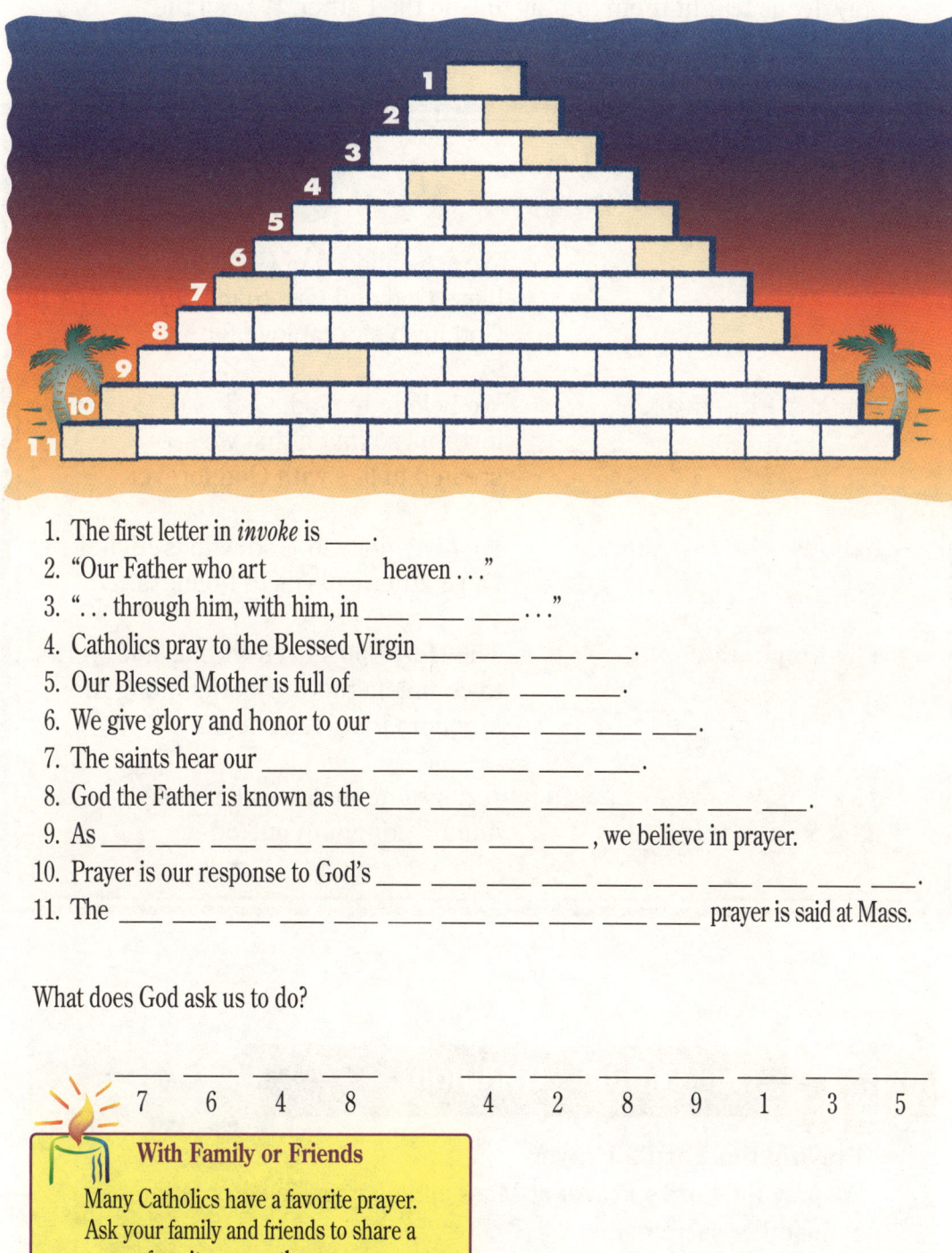

1. The first letter in *invoke* is ___.
2. "Our Father who art ___ ___ heaven . . ."
3. ". . . through him, with him, in ___ ___ ___ . . ."
4. Catholics pray to the Blessed Virgin ___ ___ ___ ___.
5. Our Blessed Mother is full of ___ ___ ___ ___ ___.
6. We give glory and honor to our ___ ___ ___ ___ ___ ___.
7. The saints hear our ___ ___ ___ ___ ___ ___ ___.
8. God the Father is known as the ___ ___ ___ ___ ___ ___ ___ ___.
9. As ___ ___ ___ ___ ___ ___ ___ ___ ___, we believe in prayer.
10. Prayer is our response to God's ___ ___ ___ ___ ___ ___ ___ ___ ___ ___.
11. The ___ ___ ___ ___ ___ ___ ___ ___ ___ ___ ___ prayer is said at Mass.

What does God ask us to do?

___ ___ ___ ___   ___ ___ ___ ___ ___ ___ ___
 7   6   4   8   4   2   8   9   1   3   5

With Family or Friends

Many Catholics have a favorite prayer. Ask your family and friends to share a favorite prayer they say.

26 The Lord's Prayer

One day when Jesus was praying, his disciples were with him. When he was finished, the disciples asked Jesus to teach them to pray. Jesus taught them to pray to God the Father. We call the prayer Jesus taught them the Lord's Prayer or the Our Father.

The Lord's Prayer	What It Means
Our Father	We are children of God. We bless God and give thanks to God for his great love for us.
who art in heaven,	We belong to God. God loves us so much that we are created to live with God forever.
hallowed be thy name.	We give glory to God who is All-holy. Our Father calls us to holiness.
Thy kingdom come.	The Holy Spirit lives with us and works to complete the work of building the kingdom that Jesus began.
Thy will be done on earth, as it is in heaven.	Jesus came to invite all people into the kingdom of God.

Our Catholic Tradition

Praying the Lord's Prayer
We pray the Lord's Prayer at Mass and during the celebration of the other sacraments.

Give us this day our daily bread,	We trust and believe that God our Father is All-knowing. He knows who we are and what we need. We, too, are to work to help people in need.
and forgive us our trespasses, as we forgive those who trespass against us,	We trust and believe that God is All-merciful and All-forgiving. God is always ready to forgive us when we are sorry. We are to treat others as God treats us. We are to forgive others.
and lead us not into temptation,	We trust and believe that the Holy Spirit is with us to help us choose what is good and avoid what is evil.
but deliver us from evil.	We trust and believe that the Holy Spirit gives us the strength to live as faithful children of God.
Amen.	We say that we believe and trust in God.

This is our Catholic faith.
Jesus taught us to pray.

 **With Family or Friends**

The people in this photo demonstrate caring and patience for one another. In what ways will you help others live the petitions in the Our Father?

REVIEW OF PART FOUR
We Pray

Match the faith terms with the descriptions in the right column.

1. _____ prayer
2. _____ prayer of blessing and adoration
3. _____ prayer of intercession
4. _____ prayer of petition
5. _____ prayer of thanksgiving
6. _____ prayer of praise
7. _____ Holy Trinity
8. _____ The Lord's Prayer

a. Praying that all people will be joined with Christ and come to know God's love for them
b. The Our Father
c. Three persons in one God
d. Acknowledging that God is God and we are children of God
e. Acknowledging God to be our Almighty Creator
f. Asking for God's forgiveness and help
g. Joining with Christ and thanking God
h. Listening and talking to God

Treasury of Catholic Prayers and Practices

Sign of the Cross

In the name of the Father,
and of the Son,
and of the Holy Spirit. Amen.

Glory Prayer

Glory to the Father,
and to the Son,
    and to the Holy Spirit:
as it was in the beginning, is now,
and will be for ever. Amen.

Prayer to the Holy Spirit

Come, Holy Spirit, fill the hearts
    of your faithful.
And kindle in them the
    fire of your love.
Send forth your Spirit and
    they shall be created.
And you will renew the
    face of the earth.

Lord's Prayer

Our Father who art in heaven,
hallowed be thy name.
Thy kingdom come.
Thy will be done on earth,
as it is in heaven.
Give us this day our daily bread,
and forgive us our trespasses,
    as we forgive those
    who trespass against us,
and lead us not into temptation,
but deliver us from evil. Amen.

Hail Mary

Hail Mary, full of grace,
the Lord is with you!
Blessed are you among women,
and blessed is the fruit
    of your womb, Jesus.
Holy Mary, Mother of God,
pray for us sinners,
now and at the hour of our death.
Amen.

Act of Contrition

My God,
I am sorry for my sins
    with all my heart.
In choosing to do wrong
and failing to do good,
I have sinned against you
whom I should love above all things.
I firmly intend, with your help,
to do penance,
to sin no more,
and to avoid whatever leads me to sin.
Our Savior Jesus Christ
suffered and died for us.
In his name, my God, have mercy.

The Apostles' Creed

I believe in God,
   the Father almighty,
   creator of heaven and earth.
I believe in Jesus Christ,
   his only Son, our Lord.
He was conceived by the
   power of the Holy Spirit
   and born of the Virgin Mary.
He suffered under Pontius Pilate,
   was crucified, died, and was buried.
   He descended into hell.
On the third day he rose again.
He ascended into heaven
   and is seated at the right
   hand of the Father.
   He will come again to judge
   the living and the dead.
I believe in the Holy Spirit,
   the holy catholic Church,
   the communion of saints,
   the forgiveness of sins,
   the resurrection of the body,
   and the life everlasting. Amen.

Grace before Meals

Bless us, O Lord,
and these your gifts
which we are about to receive
from your goodness.
Through Christ our Lord.
Amen.

Grace after Meals

Lord, give all people the food they need, so that they may join us in giving you thanks. Amen.

Rosary

Catholics pray the rosary to honor Mary and remember the important events in the life of Jesus and Mary. There are fifteen mysteries of the rosary. The word *mystery* means "the wonderful things God has done for us."

We begin praying the rosary by praying the Apostles' Creed, the Lord's Prayer, and the Hail Mary. Each mystery of the rosary is prayed by praying the Lord's Prayer once, the Hail Mary ten times, and the Glory Prayer once. When we have finished the last mystery, we pray the Hail, Holy Queen.

Joyful Mysteries

1. The Annunciation
2. The Visitation
3. The Nativity
4. The Presentation
5. The Finding of Jesus in the Temple

Sorrowful Mysteries

6. The Agony in the Garden
7. The Scourging at the Pillar
8. The Crowning with Thorns
9. The Carrying of the Cross
10. The Crucifixion

Glorious Mysteries

11. The Resurrection
12. The Ascension
13. The Coming of the Holy Spirit
14. The Assumption of Mary
15. The Coronation of Mary

Litanies

Litany is a way of praying in which a phrase of the prayer is repeated over and over again.

The Catholic Church has several litanies. They are the Litany of the Holy Name, Litany of the Sacred Heart, Litany of the Blessed Virgin Mary, Litany of Saint Joseph, and Litany of the Saints.

Litany of the Saints

Here are some petitions from the Litany of the Saints.

Lord, have mercy	Lord, have mercy
Christ, have mercy	Christ, have mercy
Lord, have mercy	Lord, have mercy
Holy Mary, Mother of God	pray for us
Saint Michael	pray for us
Holy angels of God	pray for us
Saint John the Baptist	pray for us
Saint Joseph	pray for us
Saint Peter and Saint Paul	pray for us
Saint Andrew	pray for us
Saint John	pray for us
Saint Mary Magdalene	pray for us
By your gift of the Holy Spirit	Lord, save your people
Lord Jesus, hear our prayer	Lord Jesus hear our prayer

The Divine Praises

Blessed be God.
Blessed be his holy name.
Blessed be Jesus Christ, true God and true man.
Blessed be the name of Jesus.
Blessed be his most sacred heart.
Blessed be his most precious blood.
Blessed be Jesus in the most holy sacrament of the altar.
Blessed be the Holy Spirit, the Paraclete.
Blessed be the great mother of God, Mary most holy.
Blessed be her holy and immaculate conception.
Blessed be her glorious assumption.
Blessed be the name of Mary, virgin and mother.
Blessed be Saint Joseph, her most chaste spouse.
Blessed be God in his angels and in his saints.

Hail, Holy Queen

Hail, holy Queen, mother of mercy,
hail, our life, our sweetness,
   and our hope.
To you we cry, the children of Eve;
to you we send up our sighs,
mourning and weeping
   in this land of exile.
Turn, then, most gracious advocate,
your eyes of mercy toward us;
lead us home at last
and show us the blessed fruit
   of your womb, Jesus:
O clement, O loving, O sweet
   Virgin Mary.

Stations of the Cross

1. Jesus is condemned to death.
2. Jesus accepts his cross.
3. Jesus falls the first time.
4. Jesus meets his mother.
5. Simon helps Jesus carry the cross.
6. Veronica wipes the face of Jesus.
7. Jesus falls the second time.
8. Jesus meets the women.
9. Jesus falls the third time.
10. Jesus is stripped of his clothes.
11. Jesus is nailed to the cross.
12. Jesus dies on the cross.
13. Jesus is taken down from the cross.
14. Jesus is buried in the tomb.
15. Jesus rises from the dead.

The Seven Sacraments

Sacraments of Initiation
    Baptism
    Confirmation
    Eucharist

Sacraments of Healing
    Penance
    Anointing of the Sick

Sacraments at the Service of Communion
    Holy Orders
    Matrimony

The Beatitudes

"Blessed are the poor in spirit,
    for theirs is the kingdom
        of heaven.
"Blessed are those who mourn,
    for they will be comforted.
"Blessed are the meek,
    for they will inherit the earth.
"Blessed are they who hunger
       and thirst for righteousness,
    for they will be filled.
"Blessed are the merciful,
    for they will receive mercy.
"Blessed are the pure in heart,
    for they will see God.
"Blessed are the peacemakers,
    for they will be called children
        of God.
"Blessed are those who are
       persecuted for
       righteousness' sake,
    for theirs is the kingdom
        of heaven.
"Blessed are you when people revile
       you and persecute you and
       utter all kinds of evil against
       you falsely on my account.
    Rejoice and be glad,
    for your reward is great in
       heaven." MATTHEW 5:3–12

The Ten Commandments

1. I am the LORD your God: you shall not have strange Gods before me.
2. You shall not take the name of the LORD your God in vain.
3. Remember to keep holy the LORD's Day.
4. Honor your father and your mother.
5. You shall not kill.
6. You shall not commit adultery.
7. You shall not steal.
8. You shall not bear false witness against your neighbor.
9. You shall not covet your neighbor's wife.
10. You shall not covet your neighbor's goods.

Spiritual Works of Mercy

Help people who sin.
Teach people who are ignorant.
Give advice to people who have doubts.
Comfort people who suffer.
Be patient with other people.
Forgive people who hurt you.
Pray for people who are alive and for those who have died.

Corporal Works of Mercy

Feed people who are hungry.
Give drink to people who are thirsty.
Clothe people who need clothes.
Visit prisoners.
Shelter people who are homeless.
Visit people who are sick.
Bury people who have died.

Precepts of the Church

1. Worship God at Mass with the community on Sunday and holy days of obligation, and to keep Sunday a day of rest.
2. Lead a sacramental life.
3. Study Catholic teaching.
4. Observe the marriage laws of the Church.
5. Strengthen and support the Church throughout the world.
6. Do penance, including abstaining from meat and fasting from food on the appointed days.
7. Join in the missionary spirit of the Church.

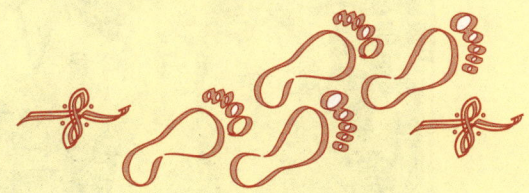

Celebrating Mass

Introductory Rites

We remember that we are the community of the Church. We prepare to listen to the word of God and to celebrate the Eucharist.

Entrance Procession and Gathering Song
We stand as the priest-presider and other ministers enter the assembly. We sing a gathering song. The priest kisses the altar. He then goes to the chair where he presides over the celebration.

Greeting
The priest leads us in praying the sign of the cross together. The priest greets us, and we say, **"And also with you."**

Penitential Rite
We admit our wrongdoings. We bless God for his mercy.

Gloria
We praise God for all the good he has done for us.

Opening Prayer
The priest leads us in praying the Opening Prayer. We respond, **"Amen."**

Liturgy of the Word

**God speaks to us today.
We listen and respond to God's word.**

First Reading
We sit and listen as the reader reads from the Old Testament or from the Acts of the Apostles. The reader concludes, "The word of the Lord." We respond, **"Thanks be to God."**

Responsorial Psalm
The song leader leads us in singing a psalm. This helps us think about what we heard in the first reading.

Second Reading
The reader reads from the New Testament, but not from the four Gospels. The reader concludes, "The word of the Lord."
We respond, **"Thanks be to God."**

Gospel Acclamation
We stand to honor Christ present with us in the gospel. The song leader leads us in singing **"Alleluia, Alleluia, Alleluia."**

Gospel
The priest or deacon proclaims, "A reading from the holy gospel according to (name of gospel writer)." We respond, **"Glory to you, Lord."** He proclaims the gospel.
At the end, he says, "The gospel of the Lord."
We respond, **"Praise to you, Lord Jesus Christ."**

Homily
We sit and think about what God is saying to us. The priest or deacon helps the whole community understand the word of God spoken to us in the readings.

Profession of Faith
We stand and profess our faith. We pray the Nicene Creed together.

General Intercessions
The priest or deacon leads us in praying for our Church and its leaders, our country and its leaders, for ourselves and others, for the sick and those who have died. We can respond to each prayer in several ways. One way we respond is, **"Lord, hear our prayer."**

Liturgy of the Eucharist

**We join with Jesus and the Holy Spirit
to give thanks and praise to God the Father.**

Preparation of the Altar and Gifts

We sit as the altar table is prepared and the collection is taken up. We share our blessings with the community of the Church and especially with those in need. The song leader may lead us in singing a song. The gifts of bread and wine are brought to the altar.

The priest lifts up the bread and blesses God for all our gifts. He prays, "Blessed are you, Lord, God of all creation . . ."

We respond, **"Blessed be God for ever."**

The priest lifts up the cup of wine and blesses God for his blessings to us. He prays, "Blessed are you, Lord, God of all creation . . ."

We respond, **"Blessed be God for ever."**

The priest invites us,
> Pray, my brothers and sisters, that our sacrifice
> may be acceptable to God, the almighty Father.

We respond,
> **May the Lord accept the sacrifice at your hands
> for the praise and
> glory of his name,
> for our good,
> and the good of all
> his Church.**

We stand and the priest leads us in praying the Prayer over the Gifts.

We respond, **"Amen."**

Eucharistic Prayer

Preface

The priest invites us to join in praying the Church's great prayer of praise and thanksgiving to God the Father.

Priest: The Lord be with you.
Assembly: And also with you.
Priest: Lift up your hearts.
Assembly: We lift them up to the Lord.
Priest: Let us give thanks to the Lord our God.
Assembly: It is right to give him thanks and praise.

Acclamation

After the priest sings the preface, we join in acclaiming,

**Holy, holy, holy Lord, God of power and might.
Heaven and earth are full of your glory.
   Hosanna in the highest.
Blessed is he who comes in the name of the Lord.
   Hosanna in the highest.**

The priest leads the assembly in praying the eucharistic prayer. We call upon the Holy Spirit to make our gifts of bread and wine holy and that they become the Body and Blood of Jesus. We recall what happened at the Last Supper. The bread and wine become the Body and Blood of the Lord. Jesus is truly and really present under the appearances of bread and wine.

Memorial Acclamation

The priest or deacon sings, "Let us proclaim the mystery of faith":
We respond, **"Christ has died, Christ is risen, Christ will come again."**
The priest prays for the Church. He prays for the living and the dead.

Doxology

The priest concludes the eucharist prayer. He sings,
   Through him, with him, in him, in the unity of the Holy Spirit,
   all glory and honor is yours, almighty Father, for ever and ever.
We respond by singing, **"Amen."**

Communion Rite

Lord's Prayer

We pray the Lord's Prayer together.

Sign of Peace

The priest invites us to share a sign of peace, saying, "The peace of the Lord be with you always." We respond, **"And also with you."** We share a sign of peace.

Breaking of the Bread

The priest breaks the host, the consecrated Bread. We sing or say,

Lamb of God, you take away the sins of the world:
   have mercy on us.
Lamb of God, you take away the sins of the world:
   have mercy on us.
Lamb of God, you take away the sins of the world:
   grant us peace.

The priest raises the host and says,

This is the Lamb of God

who takes away the sins of the world.

Happy are those who are called to his supper.

We join with him and say,

Lord, I am not worthy to receive you,
but only say the word and I shall be healed.

The priest receives Holy Communion. Next, members of the assembly receive Holy Communion. The priest or eucharistic minister holds up the host and says, "The body of Christ." We respond, **"Amen."** If we are to receive the Blood of Christ, the minister holds up the cup containing the consecrated wine and says, "The blood of Christ." We respond, **"Amen."**

Prayer after Communion

We stand as the priest invites us to pray, "Let us pray." He prays the Prayer after Communion. We respond, **"Amen."**

Concluding Rite

We are sent forth to do good works, praising and blessing the Lord.

Greeting
We stand. The priest greets us as we prepare to leave.
He says, "The Lord be with you."
We respond, **"And also with you."**

Blessing
The priest or deacon invites us,
"Bow your heads and pray for God's blessing."
The priest blesses us in the name of the Holy Trinity.
May almighty God bless you, the Father, and the Son, and the Holy Spirit.
We respond, **"Amen."**

Dismissal
The priest or deacon says, "The Mass is ended, go in peace." We respond, **"Thanks be to God."**

We sing a hymn.
The priest kisses the altar.
He and the other ministers leave in procession just as they entered.

Faith Vocabulary

A

absolution—words and blessings of the priest prayed in the sacrament of Penance that show God forgives our sins

actual grace—God's presence with us, helping us live as children of God

Advent—the season of the Church's year during which we prepare for Christmas

Anointing of the Sick—the sacrament that celebrates God's healing love

apostles—the twelve leaders Jesus chose and sent forth to continue the work he began; after Jesus' Ascension, the Church named two more apostles

Ascension of Jesus—the return of Jesus to his Father

Assumption of Mary—Mary was taken up to heaven, body and soul

B

Baptism—the sacrament in which we become members of the Church, our sins are forgiven, and we receive the gift of the Holy Spirit

Beatitudes—promises that God blesses those people who live as children of God

Bible—the written word of God

bishop—the leader of a diocese

Blessed Sacrament—the Body and Blood of Jesus, kept or reserved in the tabernacle

blessings or blessing prayers—prayers of praise and thanksgiving that remember God's presence with us

Body of Christ—the name we give to the Church and to the consecrated bread that has truly and really become Christ at Mass

C

capital sins—seven sins named by the Church that are the sources of other sins; they are pride, avarice, envy, wrath, lust, gluttony, and sloth

Catholic—a person who belongs to the Catholic Church

Catholic Church—the People of God who follow the pope and bishops as their leaders, and celebrate the seven sacraments

chrism—the blessed oil used by the Church in the celebration of the sacraments of Baptism, Confirmation, and Holy Orders

Christians—people who are baptized and believe in Jesus Christ

Christmas—the season of the Church's year that celebrates the Son of God becoming one of us; the birthday of Jesus

Church—the People of God; the community of people who believe in Jesus Christ

communion of saints—all the followers of Jesus, both the living and the dead

Confession—telling our sins to the priest in the sacrament of Penance

Confirmation—the sacrament in which we celebrate the special gift of the Holy Spirit; the sacrament that completes our Baptism

conscience—the gift of God that is part of every person and helps us know what is right and what is wrong

consecrated life—religious priests, brothers, and sisters; all the members of the Church who have taken the vows or promises of poverty, chastity, and obedience and live as members of a religious order or community

contrition—true sorrow for sin and a firm intention of not sinning

Corporal Works of Mercy—seven ways named by the Church that help us live the Great Commandment by helping others care for their physical needs

Creeds—brief summaries of what the Church believes. The two main creeds of the Church are the Apostles' Creed and the Nicene Creed.

Crucifixion of Jesus—the nailing of Jesus on the cross

D

deacons—men chosen and consecrated in the sacrament of Holy Orders to assist bishops and priests, especially in the ministry of mercy and charity

diocese—the Church in an area that is led by a bishop

Divine Providence—God caring for us and guiding us

E

Easter—the season of the Church's year that celebrates Jesus' resurrection

Easter Triduum—the three great holy days of Holy Thursday, Good Friday, and the Easter Vigil

Easter Vigil—the liturgy that commemorates the resurrection of Christ

Eucharist—the sacrament in which we share in the Body and Blood of Christ, who is truly and really present under the appearances of bread and wine

examination of conscience—thinking about and naming the choices we make and asking how they help us or do not help us live as children of God

F

faith—God's invitation to believe and trust in him. It is also our response to his invitation.

G

gifts of the Holy Spirit—seven special ways the Holy Spirit helps us live as children of God and followers of Jesus

God the Father—the first Person of the Holy Trinity

God the Son—the second Person of the Holy Trinity

God the Holy Spirit—the third Person of the Holy Trinity

Good Friday—the day we remember Jesus' dying on the cross

Gospels—the first four books of the New Testament that tell us who Jesus is and what he did for us

grace—the gift of our sharing in God's life

Great Commandment—the commandment of love of God, of others, and of ourselves

H

heaven—living with God forever

hell—a life separated from God forever after death

hierarchy—bishops, priests, and deacons—leaders of the Church who have been ordained in the sacrament of Holy Orders

Holy Communion—receiving the Body and Blood of Christ

Holy Family—Jesus, Mary, and Joseph

Holy Orders—the sacrament that celebrates a man becoming a bishop, a priest, or a deacon

Holy Sacrifice of the Mass—the Eucharist; at the Eucharist we join with Christ and praise and thank God by making Christ's sacrifice on the cross our own

Holy Spirit—the third Person of the Holy Trinity

Holy Thursday—the day we remember the Last Supper

Holy Trinity—the one God, who is three Persons—God the Father, God the Son, and God the Holy Spirit

Holy Week—the week that begins with Passion, or Palm, Sunday and ends with Easter

I

image of God—the term used in the Bible to tell us that God created us and that we share in the life of God the Father, God the Son, and God the Holy Spirit

Immaculate Conception of Mary—Mary, the mother of Jesus, was free from sin from the very first moment of her existence

incarnation—word meaning "take on flesh"; the Son of God "took on flesh," or became man; Jesus is true God and true man

J

Jesus Christ—the Son of God, who became man

K

kingdom of God—people living in peace, harmony, and respect with God, with one another, and with God's creation

L

laity—all the members of the Church who have not been ordained in the sacrament of Holy Orders

Last Supper—the meal Jesus and his disciples ate together before he died. At the Last Supper Jesus gave us the gift of his Body and Blood.

Lent—the season of the Church year that helps us get ready for Easter

liturgical year—the Church's year of seasons and feasts that celebrate and remember God's great plan of love for us

liturgy—the Church's work of worshiping God throughout the year

Liturgy of the Eucharist—the second main part of the Mass

Liturgy of the Word—the first main part of the Mass

Lord—the title used by the first Christians to show that we believe that Jesus is divine, the Son of God

Lord's Day—Sunday; the day of the resurrection of Jesus

Lord's Prayer—the Our Father, the prayer that Jesus gave us

M

magisterium—the responsibility of the pope together with the bishops to teach us the true meaning of what God has revealed and made known to us

marks of the Church—one, holy, catholic, and apostolic. The four signs, or essential qualities, of the Church founded by Jesus

Mary—the mother of Jesus; the Mother of God

Mass—the celebration of the Church at which we gather to listen to God's word and praise God at the Eucharist

Matrimony—the sacrament that unites a baptized man and woman in a lifelong bond of faithful love as a sign of Christ's love for the Church

moral virtues—the four virtues of prudence, justice, fortitude, and temperance

mortal sin—serious failure in our love and respect for God, for others, for ourselves, and for God's creation

N

New Testament—the second main part of the Bible; it tells us who Jesus is, what he did, and what he taught

O

oil of catechumens—a blessed oil used by the Church in the celebration of the sacrament of Baptism

oil of the sick—a blessed oil used by the Church in the celebration of the sacrament of Anointing of the Sick

Old Testament—the first part of the Bible; it tells us about the People of God who lived before Jesus was born

Ordinary Time—that part of the liturgical year that is not one of the seasons of Advent, Christmas, Lent, Easter Triduum, or Easter

original sin—the first sin described in the story of Adam and Eve in the Bible

Our Father—the Lord's Prayer

P

parish—the church community where Catholics come together to worship God, learn about Jesus, and work together to do what Jesus asked us to do

Paschal mystery—the death-resurrection-ascension of Jesus; the name we give to God's plan of saving us in Jesus

Passion of Jesus—Jesus' suffering and death

pastor—the leader of a parish community

Penance—a sacrament in which we celebrate God's gift of forgiveness of our sins and our reconciliation with God and with others. It is also called the sacrament of Reconciliation.

penance—satisfaction for our sins; word or action that shows we are trying to make up for our sins

Pentecost—the day that celebrates the Holy Spirit coming and living with us; the birthday of the Church

People of God—the name given to the people chosen by God to tell all people about God and how to live as God's people

pope—the leader of the whole Catholic Church; the successor of Saint Peter the Apostle

prayer—talking and listening to God

priests—men chosen and consecrated in the sacrament of Holy Orders to be co-workers with bishops

profession of faith—part of the Liturgy of the Word; the creed

Q-R

Resurrection of Jesus—the rising of Jesus from the dead

S

sacramentals—objects and prayers of the Church that remind us of God's presence and love for us and strengthen our faith in God

sacraments—seven celebrations at the center of the Church's liturgy and prayer; instituted by Jesus and allows us to share in the life and work of God

Sacraments at the Service of Communion—Holy Orders and Matrimony

Sacraments of Healing—Penance and Anointing of the Sick

Sacraments of Initiation—Baptism, Confirmation, and Eucharist

Sacred Scripture—the writings of the Bible that are God's own word to us

Sacred Tradition—the teachings of Jesus passed on to the Church by the apostles

sacrifice—doing something because of our great love for God

saints—people the Church honors because they lived a holy life. They now live with God in heaven.

sanctifying grace—the gift of God's life and love

Savior—the title we give to Jesus

sin—freely choosing to say or do what is wrong

Spiritual Works of Mercy—seven ways named by the Church that help us live the Great Commandment by helping others care for their spiritual needs

Son of God—second Person of the Holy Trinity. Jesus is the Son of God.

T

Ten Commandments—the laws God gave to Moses that guide us in living as children of God

theological virtues—faith, hope, and charity (or love)—gifts of God that give us the power to live as children of God

transubstantiation—the word we use to name our belief that the bread and wine at Mass truly and really become Jesus Christ present with us

U-V

venial sin—sin less serious than a mortal sin

virtues—habits or powers that help us do what is right and avoid what is wrong

vocation—our calling from God to serve the members of the Church and the whole world

W-Z

works of mercy—the Corporal Works of Mercy and the Spiritual Works of Mercy

worship—giving praise by our words and actions